— God's Creation Series —

OUR FATHER'S WORLD

— David K. Arwine & Michael J. McHugh —

CHRISTIAN LIBERTY PRESS • ARLINGTON HEIGHTS • ILLINOIS

Our Father's World

Ad maiorem

Dei gloriam

Christian Liberty Press
502 W. Euclid Avenue
Arlington Heights, IL 60004

www.homeschools.org

Scripture References are conformed to the Holy Bible, New King James Version ©1982, Thomas Nelson, Inc., so that modern readers may gain greater comprehension of the Word of God.

Authors: David K. Arwine & Michael J. McHugh
Editor: Edward J. Shewan
Designer: Robert Fine
Photography: Digital Stock, Robert Fine, James E. Dau,
              Corel, Artville, Photo Disc
Graphics: Christopher Kou
Cover Photo: Robert Fine

Printed in the United States of America

ISBN 1-930092-05-9

— PREFACE —

A true study of science is nothing less than an investigation of God's handiwork. The book that follows will help young children to be better equipped to explore the wonders of God's creation.

As young people study the world God made, they will discover many wonderful facts about their Creator. They will learn that their Maker is all-powerful, wise, caring, and a lover of beauty. In other words, the works of God will teach students a great deal about the nature of the great Lord of creation.

Although it is important to learn the facts of science, it is even more vital to know why God made all things. The Lord made all things for His glory. As a result, the only proper response to a study of God's creation is worship and praise. May the Creator grant each reader the desire to study the wonders of science to the glory of God.

Michael J. McHugh
Arlington Heights, Illinois
2000

— Contents —

— Chapter 1 —

GOD MADE EVERYTHING

The Lord God spoke and created everything in heaven and on earth. He did all of this in six days. This is why God alone is the great **Creator**. All **glory** belongs to God for the great things He has made.

In the beginning God created the heavens and the earth.

GENESIS 1:1

Days of Creation

Learn the song below. It teaches what God made on each of the six days of creation. Ask your teacher to help you memorize this song. Sing it to the tune of "The Twelve Days of Christmas."

On the _____ day of creation the Lord God did make the …

first	*heavens, earth, and light*
second	*sky between the waters*
third	*dry land, **seas**, and plants*
fourth	*sun, the moon, and stars*
fifth	*fish, sea creatures, and birds*
sixth	*land animals and man*

On the seventh day of creation, the Lord God did rest, and all things made were very good.

On the first day of cre-a-tion the Lord God did

make the hea-vens, earth, and light.

God is so powerful that He made the **universe**—the heavens and the earth—in only six days! He did not need years and years to create everything because God is very wise and strong.

When God finished His work, the Bible says that everything He made was *very good* (Genesis 1:31). The great Creator God was happy that He made a wonderful world.

As God's creatures, we must be sure to worship Him as the great Creator. Thank God that He made the heavens, the earth, and everything in it.

Words to Know

Creator—the One who made all things; God

glory—praise and honor given to the Lord God

seas—huge areas of water; oceans

universe—the heavens and the earth; all that God created

Looking Back

On the line at the left, write the number of the day of creation that tells when these things were made:

__2__ the sky between the waters

__6__ land animals and man

__5__ the fish, sea creatures, and birds

__4__ the sun, the moon, and the stars

__1__ the heavens, the earth, and the light

__3__ dry land, seas, and plants

In the blanks below, write the word or words that complete each sentence:

1. God made the universe in __6__ days.

2. On the seventh day of creation, God __rested__.

3. After God finished His work, the Bible says that everything that He made was __Very good__.

Chapter 2

GOD MADE THE DAY AND THE NIGHT

And God said,
Let there be light:
and there was light.
And God saw the light,
that it was good: and God
divided
the light from the darkness.
And God called the light Day,
and the darkness
He called Night.

GENESIS 1:3-5

Daytime and Nighttime

The earth is turning all the time. It **rotates** or turns all the way around every 24 hours. Do you feel the earth turning? No, the earth turns smoothly and steadily.

The sun is always shining. It gives light. You cannot see the light all the time. The sun only shines on one half of the earth at a time. When the sun shines on your part, it is daytime. God named the light "Day."

When it is dark, you can see the moon and stars. Where did the sun go? It is not shining on your part of the earth. The Earth has turned away from the sun. It is nighttime. The earth turns and turns. Soon it will be daytime again. God named the darkness "Night."

6

The Sun

Then God made two great lights: the greater light to rule the day....

GENESIS 1:16A

The sun is very big. It is larger than a million earths. Why does the sun look so small? It looks small because it is very far away. For the same reason, a big airplane looks small when it is flying overhead.

The sun is very bright. DO NOT look at the sun directly; it will hurt your eyes. You may become blind.

On a sunny day, you can see your shadow. Do you know what a shadow is? If you go outside, you can see the dark shape of your body on the ground. Your body blocks out the sunlight and makes a shadow.

The Moon

Then God made two
great lights: ... the
lesser light to rule
the night....

GENESIS 1:16B

The sun shines on the earth and gives us light. The sun also shines on the **moon**. At night, when there are no clouds in the sky, you can see the moon shining. It gets its light from the sun. Sometimes you can even see the moon during the day.

The moon is smaller than the earth. On the moon, it is very hot in the morning and very cold at night. There is no air or water on the moon. The mountains and craters make it look like the moon has a face.

Has anyone ever been to the moon? Yes! In 1969, two men from the United States took a **spaceship** there. They were the first ones to walk on the moon. Maybe someday you will travel there and learn more about this moon God made.

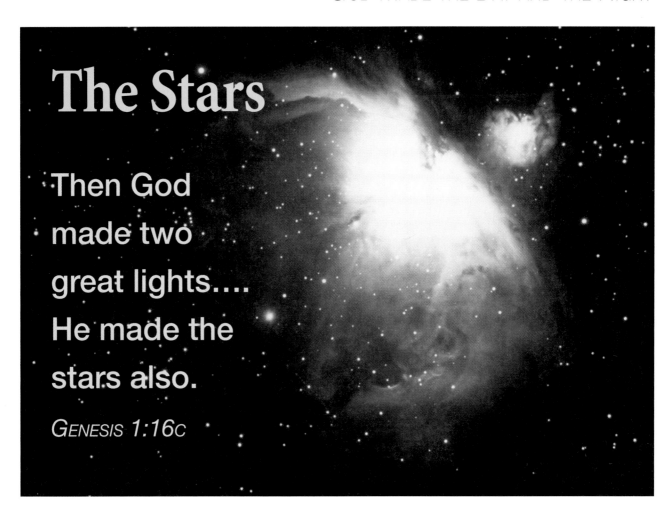

The Stars

Then God
made two
great lights....
He made the
stars also.

GENESIS 1:16c

At night, the sky is dark and you can see the stars. Can you see stars during the day? No! The sun makes the sky so bright that you cannot see them. If you have a flashlight, shine it at night and during the day. When is it easier to see? Why?

Can you always see the stars at night? No, you cannot see them when it is cloudy. On a clear night, though, you can see many stars; but you cannot see all of them with your eyes. Some are too far away. If you have a telescope, it can help you see them.

How many stars are there? Only God knows how many there are. Some people who study the stars say that there are billions of them. Stars are very far from the earth; but the closer they are to us, the brighter they look.

Some stars make pictures in the sky. If you look up in the sky at night, maybe you can see some of these pictures. Can you find the **Big Dipper**?

Stars in the Northern Sky

The heavens declare the glory of God; and the firmament shows His handiwork.

PSALM 19:1

SOMETHING YOU CAN DO

You will *need*: a ball, a flashlight, and a postage stamp.

Pretend the ball is the Earth, the flashlight is the Sun, and the stamp is where you live. Place the stamp on the ball. Turn off the lights in the room and shine the flashlight on the ball. Now turn the ball slowly. Watch the stamp as you turn the ball. When is it day? When is it night? When do you see the sunlight?

Words to Know

rotate—to turn in a circle or spin

moon—a heavenly body that circles a planet

planet—a huge heavenly body that moves around the sun

spaceship—a ship that flies high into outer space

Big Dipper—a star picture of a cup (or dipper)

Tell your teacher the correct answer to the following questions.

1. How long does it take the earth to turn all the way around?

2. Can you feel the earth turn?

3. Does the sun always shine?

4. What is day?

5. What is night?

6. Is the sun bigger or smaller than the earth?

7. How does the Moon get its light?

8. Why are you unable to see the stars during the day?

9. How many stars are there?

—Chapter 3—
GOD MADE SEASONS

And God said, Let there be lights in the
firmament of the heaven to divide the day from
the night; and let them be for signs, and for
seasons, and for days, and years.

— GENESIS 1:14 —

God Made Four Seasons

The Bible teaches us that God made days by giving us a time of light and darkness. God also made seasons so each year would have four parts. Each **season** of the year has about 90 days or three months.

God made each **year** with four parts. We call each part a season. Try to learn the name of each season:

Winter	January	February	March
Spring	April	May	June
Summer	July	August	September
Fall	October	November	December

God's Special Plan for Each Season

WINTER

SPRING

SUMMER

FALL

And God said, Let there be lights in the firmament of the heaven to divide the day from the night: and let them be for signs, and for seasons, and for days, and years.

GENESIS 1:14

The Earth Rests During the Winter

WINTER

Winter is a time for God's creation to rest and repair.

The days of winter are colder than the other seasons. Plants rest or grow very slowly during the winter. The sun does not shine as strongly during wintertime. The trees, grass, and other plants rest and wait for spring to come.

God giveth snow like wool:
He scattereth the frost like ashes.

PSALM 147:16

The Earth Comes Alive in Spring

SPRING

Spring is a time when living things can shine.

In springtime the earth comes alive. The days begin to get warmer and longer. Spring comes after the cold winter season. God often sends rain to help His creation come alive in springtime.

In spring, the grass begins to grow. Farmers plant their seeds. People watch pretty flowers begin to bloom. God gives new life to His creation.

Summer Gives Brightness and Warmth

SUMMER

The sun shines long and hard during the summer.

Summer is filled with hot sunny days. People like to work and play outdoors during the summertime. Plants grow fast in the summer months. Living things need sunshine and water to grow well.

While the earth remaineth, seedtime and harvest, and cold and heat, and summer and winter, and day and night shall not cease.

GENESIS 8:22

Fall Days are Shorter and Cooler

Fall is a time
to gather treasures
from God's creation.

The fall season is a busy time. Food needs to be picked from the fields before the cold wintertime begins. Leaves need to be raked before the snow comes.

As fall settles in, the earth begins to grow colder and darker. The sun does not shine as strongly as it did during the summertime.

SOMETHING YOU CAN DO

Ask your teacher to help you keep a **weather** chart. This chart will teach you how the weather changes each day of a month. Write the correct number for each day in the month on the **calendar** that follows. Begin watching the weather on the first day of the month.

Look at the sky each morning. Is the weather sunny, cloudy, rainy, or snowy? Ask your teacher to help you understand each weather picture below. After you look at the sky, draw on the chart the picture that best shows the weather.

After you have finished your chart, tell your teacher which season of the year this month fell on. How many days were sunny? cloudy? rainy? snowy? How does watching the weather help you know what clothes to wear? what you can do outside?

Words to Know

firmament—the sky or heaven above the earth

season—one of the four parts of a year; spring, summer, fall, or winter; each season is about 90 days or three months

year—the passing of twelve months or the four seasons

weather—what it is like outside; sunny, cloudy, rainy, or snowy

calendar—a chart that shows the days, weeks, and months of one year

Weather Chart for the Month of:

_____

GOD MADE SEASONS

SUN	MON	TUES	WED	THUR	FRI	SAT

Looking Back

Circle true or false:

1. God gave us four seasons.   true   false

2. Each season lasts the whole year.   true   false

3. Our seasons are winter, spring, summer, and fall.   true   false

4. The spring season is very hot and dry.   true   false

5. It is very dark for most of the summer.   true   false

6. Fall is the time for gathering food from the fields.   true   false

7. Winter is filled with hot sunny days.   true   false

8. Most plants rest during the winter season.   true   false

— Chapter 4 —
GOD MADE PLANTS

And God said, Let the earth bring forth grass,
the herb yielding seed, and the fruit tree yielding
fruit after his kind, whose seed is in itself,
upon the earth: and it was so.

GENESIS 1:11-12

23

Understanding Plants

God created plants for our good. Without them we cannot live. Plants help us in many ways. They give us food, clothing, **fuel**, and much more. Plants are beautiful too. The more we learn about plants, the more we learn about the wise Creator.

STRANGE PLANTS

The sundew is a very strange plant that grows in the southern United States. It has sweet-smelling honey which attracts insects. But they are in for a surprise when they try to get the honey, because it is so sticky they can't get away. Then the plant slowly closes up and eats THEM!

What Are Plants Like?

Some plants are big and some are small. A tree is a big plant and grass is a little one. Plants are living things. People and animals are living things, too; but most plants cannot move like people and animals move. Plants stay in one place.

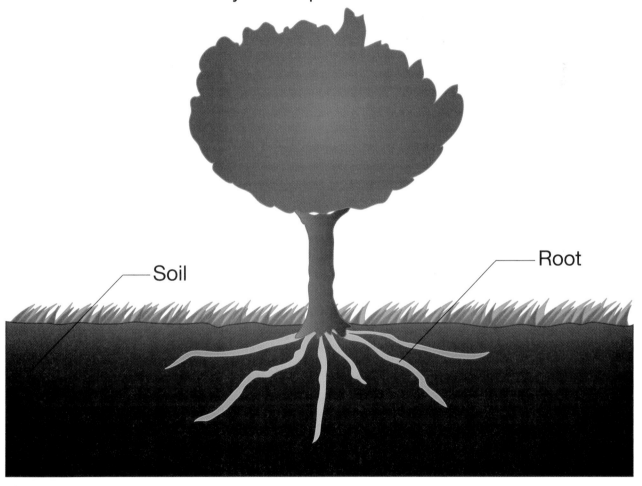

Soil

Root

Plants get water and food from the ground. Do you know how plants do this? Plants have **roots** that grow down into the **soil** and pull up the water and food they need. This helps them to grow strong and healthy. The sun also helps plants to make food.

25

Why Are Plants So Important?

If a cow could talk she might answer, "If I did not eat grass, I could not make milk for my calf."

A bird might answer, "I need a tree in which to build a nest and plants to make the nest."

A bee might answer, "I need pretty flowers to help me make honey."

If God did not make plants on the earth, animals could not live. They need to eat plants as their food. Some animals also need plants to build the homes in which they live. God was very wise when He made all kinds of plants.

Plants Help People Too

• People use the fruit of plants for food.

• People use cotton from cotton plants to make clothes.

• People make some plants into **medicine**.

• People also use wood from trees for making buildings.

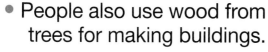

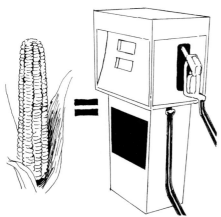

• People even make corn into fuel for automobiles.

The Four Main Parts of a Plant

The four main parts of a plant are the **roots**, the **stem**, the **leaves**, and the **flower**. Ask your teacher to help you write the correct name of each part in the picture below.

Many Plants Are Grown for Food

Many plants are good to eat. What parts of the plant do we eat?

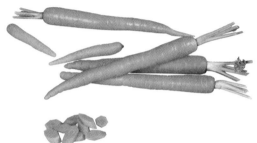

We eat the root of the carrot plant.

We eat the stem of the asparagus plant.

We eat the leaves of the lettuce plant.

These plant parts are called vegetables. Have you ever seen a vegetable garden? Maybe you can start one of your own! If you do, be sure to water the plants and pull the weeds. The plants will need plenty of sunshine, too. It is fun to watch the plants grow.

Flowers and Fruit

Do you eat flowers? No, but some flowers turn into **fruit**. Not every flower becomes fruit, though. God made some just for us to enjoy. They are beautiful. Flowers come in all shapes, sizes, and colors; they smell good too.

What is your favorite flower?

Fruit is very good to eat. Fruit helps us to grow strong and healthy. It also comes in all shapes, sizes, and colors; it tastes good too. What is your favorite fruit? Many boys and girls enjoy apples, oranges, bananas, and watermelon.

Draw a picture of your favorite fruit and your favorite flower in the spaces below.

My Favorite Fruit

My Favorite Flower

Where Do Plants Come From?

Most plants come from **seeds**. Seeds are made by the flower of a plant. After the seeds are fully grown, they are placed into the soil to start new plants. The seeds die and new plants begin to grow. Water

and sunlight helps them grow big and strong.

If we plant a corn seed in some soil, what kind of plant will grow? Yes, a corn plant will grow. Each plant has a special kind of seed that makes another one just like itself. God made seeds this way so that we would always have that kind of plant in the world.

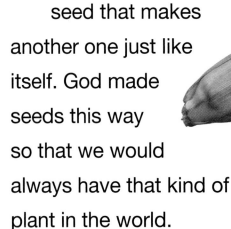

Seeds Are Good to Eat

We do not always use seeds to start new plants. Sometimes we use them as food. Wheat, corn, and oats are seeds used in many of the cereals we eat for breakfast. What are some other seeds we eat? Peanuts, beans, and walnuts are just a few.

We are not the only ones that eat seeds, though. Animals eat seeds too. Many farm animals eat corn and other

seeds. Have you ever seen birds eat seeds? Seeds come in all shapes and sizes. Why, did you know that even popcorn is a seed?

How Do Seeds Travel?

Do you ever wonder how plants begin to grow if no one planted them? You learned that plants come from seeds; but how did those seeds get to the place where they are growing? Did you know that seeds can travel? They travel in many different ways.

One way is by the wind. Have you ever seen a dandelion after it turns white? The fluffy white parts carry the seeds into the air. If you blow on them, what will happen? The seeds will begin to float. These seeds travel in the air until they land in a new place.

Seeds can also travel on people and animals. Look! Something is on your sock. What is it? It is a bur. A bur is a seed that sticks to anything that brushes against it. You may give it a ride to its new home. Soon it will fall off and begin to grow a new plant.

Burs come in all shapes and sizes

Another way seeds can travel is on water. Some seeds fall into a lake, pond, or river, and they float away. Sometimes people or animals drop seeds in the water too. When the seeds reach land, some begin to grow new plants in their new home.

SOMETHING YOU CAN DO

Things you will need:

ten corn seeds, ten bean seeds, two glass jars (1 quart pickle jars are good for this), potting soil, two glasses half full of water

Place the bean seeds in one glass of water and the corn seeds in the other. Let them sit overnight. Next, take out a seed and carefully open it. What do you see? Can you see the new plant inside? The rest of the seed is used as food for the baby plant.

Now fill the glass jars half full with potting soil. Make little holes with your finger against the side of the jar. Gently plant the corn seeds in one jar and the bean seeds in the other. Keep the soil in the jars moist by watering it lightly every day.

Place the jars near a window for sunlight. Wait seven days. What happened? Has a tiny plant appeared? Wait another four days and check your plants. Wait another four days and compare the two kinds of plants. Which plants are bigger, the corn or the beans?

Tell your teacher how the corn plants are different from the bean plants. Can you name the parts of these plants?

God's Beautiful World

When I look at the world
It is easy to see,
What a beautiful place
God made for me.

Down in the meadows
Are flowers so fair
God clothed them in beauty
A king could not share.

Out in the forest
I hear in the trees,
The music of God
In the rustling leaves.

When I look at the world
It is easy to see,
Plants are a gift
God has given to me.

ACTIVITY

Ask your parents to buy a small birdfeeder and a small bag of birdseed. Put this birdfeeder in your yard or a park near your home. Each day write down how many kinds of birds visit your birdfeeder. You could also draw a picture of each bird you see.

Words to Know

fuel—something that burns which creates heat or power; wood, coal, oil, or gas (all come from plants)

roots—the part of a plant that grows down into the soil

soil—ground that is made of tiny bits of rock and dead plants

medicine—something that helps people get better when they are sick

stem—the part of a plant that grows above the soil and holds the leaves, flowers, and fruit

leaves—green parts of a plant that grow out of the stem; they make food for the plant and help it "breathe"

flower—the colorful part of a plant that makes the fruit

fruit—the part of a plant that can be eaten; it is made from the flower and has one or more seeds in it

seeds—parts of a plant found in the fruit; they make new plants

Looking Back

Tell your teacher the correct answer to the following questions.

1. What kind of plant can be used to make clothes?

2. What kind of plant can be used to build a house?

3. Can you name the four main parts of the plant?

4. Name some of the plant parts we eat.

5. What part of the plant makes the seeds?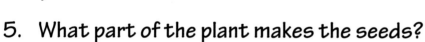

6. If people did not plant seeds, how did the plants get there?

7. Do cows eat plants? Why?

8. What is soil?

— Chapter 5 —
GOD MADE INSECTS

And God made … everything that creeps on the
earth according to its kind. And God saw
that it was good.

GENESIS 1:25B

What is an Insect?

Did you know that there are more insects in the world than there are people? There are at least a million different kinds. Not all creeping things are insects, though. A spider is not an insect because it has eight legs. Insects are animals that have six legs.

Insects are alike in many ways. They all have a hard outer covering; it is made up of three main body parts—a head, **thorax** (middle), and **abdomen** (end). All insects also have two feelers on their heads. Most insects have one or two pairs of wings.

Insects are very different in others ways. Some insects fly, some crawl, some run very fast, and some can even swim. Some flying insects cannot walk and other insects live under the ground for years. Some insects live in groups and others like to live alone.

So, the next time you see an insect, try and find out what kind it is. God made them all for a special purpose.

40

Insect Body Parts

An insect has three main body parts. Do you remember what they are? They are the head, thorax (middle part), and the abdomen (end part).

Study the insect below and label its parts.

Some Insects Harm Man

Termites are insects that eat wood. They can damage furniture and houses made of wood. The moth ruins clothes and the roach eats books. Other insects, like mosquitoes and fleas, carry **diseases**, that make people very sick.

Termites look like ants, and eat wood.

Locusts are insects that eat leaves and other plant parts; they look much like grasshoppers. Locusts travel in groups. Together they can eat a farmer's entire crop in minutes. Do you know where you can read about them in the Bible? (Exodus 10:1–20)

Mosquitoes can make people sick.

Locusts look like grasshoppers.

He spake, and the locusts came, and caterpillars, and that without number, and did eat up all the herbs in their land, and devoured the fruit of their ground.

PSALMS 105:34-35

Some Insects Help Man

The praying mantis eats many other insects, including flies and mosquitoes.

The mantid, or praying mantis, is an insect that helps the farmer; it eats other insects that ruin his crops.

Butterflies carry **pollen** from one flower to another. This helps the flowers to make seeds.

The honeybee gathers nectar from flowers and turns it into honey. Do you like to eat honey?

Another insect helps man make beautiful cloth out of **silk**. Silk is soft, shiny thread that is made by the silkworm.

How Do Insects Protect Themselves?

Insects are food for many animals, but God gave each one a special gift. Insects use these gifts to keep from being eaten.

Some insects are the same color or shape of the things around them. For example, the katydid is green like the leaves on which it lives. This makes it very hard for its enemies to see it.

The katydid's color helps keep it safe.

God made the walking stick to look like a twig so it can hide on branches. Unless it moves, you might not see it at all.

The cockroach has the gift of speed. When it is scared, it runs away very quickly, so its enemies cannot catch it.

Many insects simply fly away, but the wasp fights back! If you make the wasp mad, it will give you a very painful sting. Ouch!

Without these special gifts, insects could not protect themselves. God was very wise when He made the insects.

44

Some Insects Change as They Grow

Almost all insects lay eggs. For example, the mosquito lays its eggs in the water. After they hatch, the baby mosquitoes go through many changes before they are old enough to grow wings and fly away. What do these changes look like?

Study this picture.

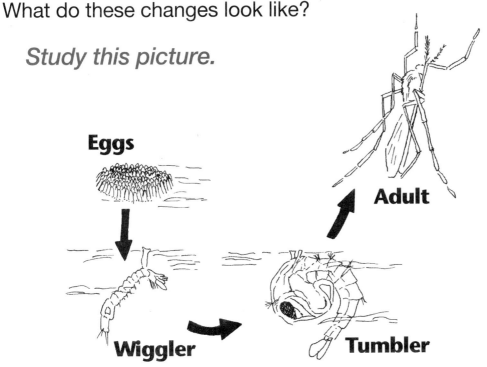

First the mosquito lays its eggs. Next the eggs hatch and out come **wigglers**; they swim and eat tiny plants in the water. Then the wigglers turn into **tumblers** which are still active. Last, they break out of their coverings as adult mosquitoes and fly away.

Butterflies are Born Twice!

Butterflies are insects that also go through many changes. Each kind of butterfly is different, but the Monarch is one of the most famous and easiest to study.

In the spring, they lay their eggs on the leaves of milkweed plants. Soon the eggs hatch into little **caterpillars**. The caterpillars will spend most of the summer eating and eating. During this time, they will grow big and plump.

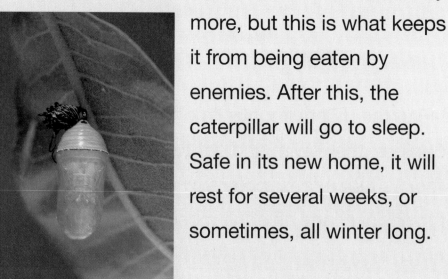

Then, each caterpillar attaches itself to a twig or leaf and sheds its skin. Then the new skin underneath changes into a hard shell called a **chrysalis**. It doesn't even look like an insect any more, but this is what keeps it from being eaten by enemies. After this, the caterpillar will go to sleep. Safe in its new home, it will rest for several weeks, or sometimes, all winter long.

Then one day, the chrysalis will become clear enough to see through it, and then it will split open. Do you know what will come out? Do you think it will still be a caterpillar? No! It has changed into a beautiful butterfly! All the time the caterpillar was in the chrysalis, it was changing into an adult butterfly.

Social Insects

Some insects like to live alone; but **social insects** like to live in large groups called colonies. Ants are social insects that are so small that they cannot fight their enemies alone. Living together in **colonies**, however, makes it easier to defend themselves.

Each member of a colony has a chore to do. Soldier ants protect the colony. Worker ants build and clean their homes. The queen ant lays eggs so there will be more ants in the future. Nurse ants tend the eggs and care for the baby ants after they hatch.

Can you think of other insects that live together?

The ants are a people not strong, yet they prepare their meat in the summer....

PROVERBS 30:25

HOW ANTS GROW

Egg   Larva   Pupa Stage

Adult ant

Most ants live underground, so we don't usually see them.

However, some ants make large "buildings" above ground, called "anthills." These two "anthills" in Africa are not actually made by ants, but by termites.

Sometimes the termites are attacked by other REAL ants, which take over the anthills as their own homes.

The anthill in the photo above, has been broken open by elephants looking for salt to eat.

Because the termites used clay that contained lots of salt, the elephants broke the anthill open with their tusks.

SOMETHING YOU CAN DO

Can you keep insects as pets? Yes you can, but not all insects make good pets. A good insect to keep as a pet is the cricket. In the summer you can catch them just about anywhere. If you cannot find any, most pet stores will have them.

Crickets are safe and fun to watch. At night they chirp like little birds. How do they make this noise? They make it by rubbing their wings together very quickly. If you watch closely, you may see them do this.

Things you will need:

1) A cage (use a plastic box with a screen cover), food (ground up dog food works well), and a moist sponge

2) After you prepare the cage, place the food and a moist sponge in the box. Find a pet cricket and put it in the cage. Remember to change the food and sponge every few days. If you do this, your cricket will live long, and you will have many hours of enjoyment.

Can you find the insects in the pictures below?

Words to Know

thorax—the middle part of an insect

abdomen—the end part of an insect

disease—something that makes people very sick

pollen—yellow "dust" that flowers make; bees carry the pollen to other plants that help them grow fruit with seeds

silk—soft, shiny thread made by the silkworm or other insects

wigglers—baby mosquitoes

tumblers—young mosquitoes

caterpillars—baby butterflies

chrysalis—a special "home" made by a caterpillar where it rests and changes into a butterfly

social insects—insects that like to live together in large groups

colonies—large groups of social insects

Looking Back

Tell your teacher the correct answer to the following questions.

1. Are there more insects or people in the world?

2. How many legs does an insect have?

3. Is the locust a good insect? Why or why not?

4. How is a praying mantis helpful to farmers?

5. Name an insect that hides from its enemies on green leaves.

6. Where do mosquitoes lay their eggs?

7. What do caterpillars become?

8. What are the three main parts of an insect?

9. Do ants live together or apart? Why?

— Chapter 6 —
GOD MADE ANIMALS

And God said,
Let the earth
bring forth the
living creature
after his kind, cattle,
and creeping thing;
and beast of the
earth after his kind,
and it was so.

GENESIS 1:24

What are Animals?

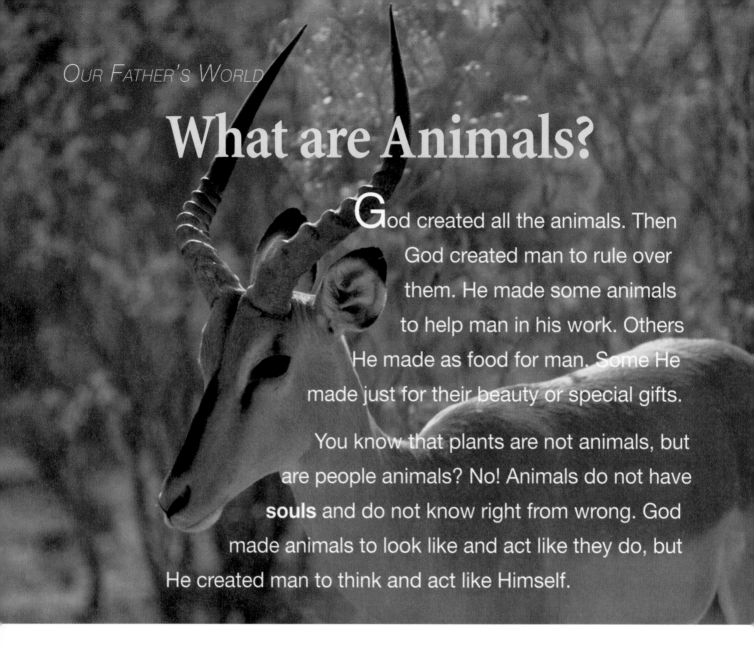

God created all the animals. Then God created man to rule over them. He made some animals to help man in his work. Others He made as food for man. Some He made just for their beauty or special gifts.

You know that plants are not animals, but are people animals? No! Animals do not have **souls** and do not know right from wrong. God made animals to look like and act like they do, but He created man to think and act like Himself.

As we study animals we will begin to learn more about the wonders of God's creation.

And out of the ground the Lord God formed every beast of the field, and every fowl of the air; and brought them to Adam to see what he would call them: and whatsoever Adam called every living creature, that was the name thereof.

Genesis 2:19

Some Animals Go on Vacation

Wintertime is often very cold in North America. At this time, many people take a vacation and go south where it is warm. Did you know that many animals do the same thing?

When you are playing outside in the snow, do you ever see a swallow? No, swallows go south in the winter. It is warm there, and food is easy to find. When spring comes, the swallow appears again. It has come back to its home in the north.

When animals go on vacation in the winter, we say they **migrate**. It is a gift that God has given, not only to birds, but also to monarch butterflies, whales, and other animals. If they do not migrate, many of these animals might die.

Even the stork in the heavens knows her appointed times; and the turtledove, the swift, and the swallow observe the time of their coming....

JEREMIAH 8:7A

Some Animals Sleep All Winter Long

In the fall, most plants begin to dry up and die. You learned that many animals migrate when this happens. Some animals, however, stay behind. If their food dries up, what do they eat? How do they keep warm? God has given them a different gift.

Have you ever watched a squirrel in the fall? It is always running from place to place. What is it looking for? Why is it so busy? The squirrel knows that winter is coming, and it must find as much food as it can before it takes its long winter nap.

God lets it **hibernate**. What does hibernate mean? It means that some animals find a warm, dry place where they can go to sleep all winter long. When spring comes and the sun begins to warm the earth, these animals wake up and go out to find fresh food.

Can you think of any other animals that hibernate?

Some Animals Must Hunt

As you have learned, some animals hibernate and others migrate during the winter. But do all animals do this? No, many animals stay and **forage**. What does forage mean? It means to look hard for food.

If they do not look for food, they might die.

The deer is an animal that forages. It lives through the winter by eating little bunches of grass that poke up through the snow. They also like to munch on acorns. If they cannot find grass or acorns, they will eat the tender bark or twigs from a tree.

The wolf is another animal that forages. It lives through the winter by hunting other animals. Can you think of a kind of bird that forages by eating other animals? An eagle is a bird that looks hard for small animals, like mice and squirrels, to eat.

"Also, to every beast of the earth, to every bird of the air, and to everything that creeps on the earth, in which there is life, I have given every green herb for food"; and it was so.

GENESIS 1:30

QUESTIONS ABOUT ANIMALS

Fill in the boxes.

Write whether the animal

hibernates, migrates, or forages.

Animal Homes

People live in many different kinds of houses, and animals do too. Their houses are not exactly like ours, but they are alike in some ways.

● Some people like to live in an apartment building. But did you know that some animals also like to live in a place just like that? The purple martin is a bird that lives in an "apartment building." It lives in a room or "apartment" next to other purple martins. Their "apartment building" is called a birdhouse.

● Some people like to live in a mobile home. Do you know any animals that like to live in a place like that? Yes, the turtle carries around its "mobile home" wherever it goes; it is called a shell. Can you think of other animals that like to live in shells? (snails)

● Some people like to live in a house that is made of stone. Some animals also like to live in stone houses. Bats live in a stone house called a cave. They sleep all day long and then, at night, come out to feed on harmful insects. Bats are helpful to people.

And Jesus said to him, "Foxes have holes and birds of the air have nests, but the Son of Man has nowhere to lay His head."

MATTHEW 8:20

59

City Dwellers

Some people like to live in a big skyscraper. Termites from Africa are animals that also like to live in a place like that! They build large anthills, or "skyscrapers," with bits of plants and soil.

Many of these mounds are taller than you are! They even have a way to keep their homes cool in hot weather. You may have hundreds of neighbors, but the African termite has millions.

Put an X over those things that animals use for houses.

60

"Playing Possum"

What is Rusty barking at? Look over there. What is it? It looks like a big mouse. Rusty has found an animal called an opossum. Is it dead? No, it is just "playing dead" so Rusty will leave him alone. If it lies real still, Rusty will think it is dead and leave it.

After Rusty leaves, the opossum will get up and walk away. This is called "**playing possum**." God gave the opossum this gift so that it could protect itself from other animals. Do you know of other animals that use this gift? (hognose snake, weevil, mouse)

Animal Tracks

When it is raining or snowing outside, do you like making footprints in the mud or snow? Animals also leave footprints in mud and snow. We call these footprints **tracks**.

Can you tell what kind of animal has left tracks? First you must first learn something about the feet of the animals that left them.

These funny looking tracks in the snow were made by a wild turkey, as it was looking for food in the winter.

The wild turkey

Animal Feet

Among the beasts, whatever divides the hoof,
having cloven **hooves** and chewing the cud
—that you may eat.

LEVITICUS 11:3

The deer is an animal that has hard hooves.
They leave a track that looks like this:

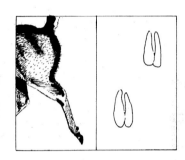

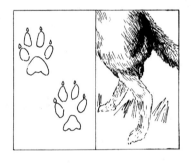

Dogs and wolves have padded feet so they can
walk quietly. They leave tracks that look like this:

God gave the duck
webbed feet. Why do you think He did this?
God created the duck to spend a lot of time in
the water. The duck leaves a track like this:

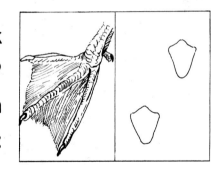

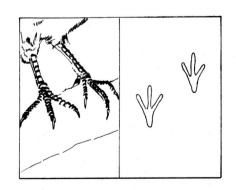

Count your toes. How many do you have?
Most birds have only three. Some birds leave
tracks like this:

SOMETHING YOU CAN DO

Ask your teacher to take you outside to find some animal tracks. You may have to look carefully. After you have found a few, try to tell your teacher from what kind of animal they came. You may want to make plaster castings of the tracks, too.

In the box below, draw one of the animal tracks you found.

I found the tracks of a: _____

Words to Know

soul—the spirit of a person that lives forever

migrate—when some animals travel to warmer places during the winter to find food

hibernate—when some animals sleep all winter long

forage—to look hard for food

"playing possum"—when an animal pretends to be dead; it protects itself from its enemies by doing this

tracks—the "footprints" that animals make in the mud or snow

hooves—the "feet" of some animals like deer, cows, and sheep

65

Looking Back

Circle true or false:

1. Man and animals are the same.   true   false

2. Hibernate means to sleep all during the winter.   true   false

3. Forage means to look hard for food.   true   false

4. Turtles do not have shells.   true   false

5. Tracks are footprints left by animals.   true   false

6. Most deer have webbed feet.   true   false

7. Ducks have webbed feet.   true   false

8. A deer has feet called hooves.   true   false

— Chapter 7 —

GOD MADE PEOPLE

And God said,
"Let Us make man in Our image,
according to Our likeness; let them
have **dominion** over the fish of the sea,
over the birds of the air, and over the cattle,
over all the earth and over every creeping thing
that creeps on the earth." So God created man in His
own image; in the image of God He created him;
male and female He created them.

GENESIS 1:26-27

God's Plan for His People

God made the world and He made people to live on it. The Lord put people on the earth to love and serve Him. This was a part of His plan. God has a plan for everything He has made, and that includes you.

You are a part of God's plan. He wants you to love and serve Him. God the Creator also wants you to learn more about Him and His creation. This is why He has given you a wonderful body, mind, and soul.

When you were a tiny baby, you could not learn much about God's world. Now you are older, and God wants you to learn as much as possible about everything He has made. But how do you learn about God's creation?

God has given you eyes to see, ears to hear, a tongue to taste, skin to feel, and a nose to smell to help you learn about His world. These things are called your **five senses**. He wants you to use them wisely as you grow and learn.

Write these five senses in the space below.

1. *eyes to* _____

2. *ears to* _____

3. *a tongue to* _____

4. *skin to* _____

5. *a nose to* _____

69

The Sense of Sight

God made you to see with your eyes. He expects you to make good use of them. If you carefully look at the things around you, you are studying God's creation. When you study God's creation, it is called **science**.

List 5 things that you can see in this picture.

1.＿＿＿＿＿＿＿＿＿＿＿＿＿＿＿

2.＿＿＿＿＿＿＿＿＿＿＿＿＿＿＿

3.＿＿＿＿＿＿＿＿＿＿＿＿＿＿＿

4.＿＿＿＿＿＿＿＿＿＿＿＿＿＿＿

5.＿＿＿＿＿＿＿＿＿＿＿＿＿＿＿

Your eyes help you in many ways. They help you see shapes like circles and squares. They also help you see many kinds of things and people. They help you see colors, too. How many kinds of colors can you see with your eyes?

SOMETHING YOU CAN DO

Look at the toys in the picture below. There are many wonderful toys for children to buy. Now look at the big picture very carefully for about three minutes.

After you are done studying the picture, write down as many toys as you can remember without looking. You have only five minutes to do this. How many did you remember?

Games to Play

What is under the Towel?

You can play this game with one or more of your friends. Ask your mom or dad to collect small things from around your home. Your parent should then place them on the kitchen table and cover them with a towel. Don't peek!

After the table is ready, each player will sit down and the towel will be removed. You will have one minute to carefully look at all the objects. When the time is done, cover them again. Write down as many things as you can remember. Whoever remembers the most objects is the winner.

Look and Remember

Sit at the kitchen table, and look around the room. Carefully note where everything is placed. After three minutes, leave the room. Ask your mom or dad to move around some of the things, like the coffeemaker, toaster, and clock in the kitchen.

Return to the kitchen when your mom or dad is done. Each player should then write down all the things that were changed in the room. The winner will be the one who has written down the most changes.

Safety First

The Lord wants you to take good care of your eyes.

You only get one set of eyes!

Remember:

1. Never put anything into your eyes. If you are working or playing around flying objects, be sure to wear safety glasses or something to protect your eyes.

2. DO NOT look directly at the sun. You may go blind!

3. Always read with plenty of light so your eyes do not get tired.

4. Visit an eye doctor once each year so he can check your eyes and keep them healthy.

The Sense of Hearing

You can hear with your ears. God wants you to hear things.

So then faith comes by hearing, and hearing by the Word of God.
Romans 10:17

List 5 sounds that you hear each day.

1._____

2._____

3._____

4._____

5._____

Your ears help you in many ways. They help you understand what other people are saying. They help you know what is going on around you, so you know how to act. They can also help by warning you of possible danger.

The Lord wants you to take good care of your ears. You only get one pair of ears!

Remember:

1. Never put anything into your ears. If you are working around loud noises, be sure to protect your ears with earplugs or earphones.

2. Never shout, make a loud noise, or pop a balloon near a person's ear.

3. Be sure to clean your ears very carefully each week. During cold weather, be sure to wear a warm hat over your ears.

4. Visit a doctor each year so he can check your ears and keep them healthy.

75

The Sense of Taste

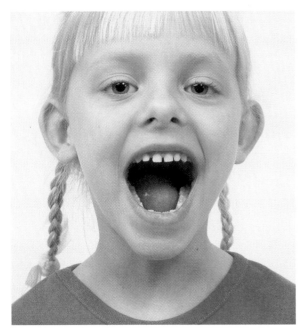

You can taste with your tongue. God wants you to taste things.

Your tongue can tell you if food is too hot for your mouth.

List 5 kinds of food that you have tasted.

1. _____

2. _____

3. _____

4. _____

5. _____

God made your tongue in a special way. It can tell if something is salty, sour, bitter, or sweet.

SOMETHING YOU CAN DO

Ask your teacher to collect food that is sweet, bitter, sour, and salty. Then cover your eyes with a blindfold and have your teacher give you one kind of food to taste at a time. After tasting each kind, say if it is sweet, bitter, sour, or salty.

God wants you to eat things that are good. You must be very careful what you put in your mouth.

Remember:

1. Never put anything in your mouth except good food. Do not eat things that are stale or have been left out for a long time.

2. Do not take things from the medicine cabinet to taste.

3. Do not try to chew things that are too hard. Some children break their teeth by chewing on hard candy or ice.

The Sense of Feeling

You can feel with your skin.
God wants you to feel things.

List 5 different kinds of things you can feel with your fingers:

1._____

2._____

3._____

4._____

5._____

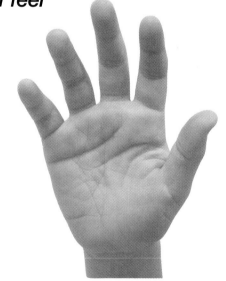

God made your skin in a special way. It protects your body and helps you to feel many different things.

SOMETHING TO DO

Have your teacher put a blindfold over your eyes so you cannot see anything. Then let your teacher give you different things to feel. Tell what each object is like.

See if you can tell which objects are smooth or rough, hot or cold, wet or dry, round or square, soft or hard, or heavy rather than light.

smooth or rough

hot or cold

wet or dry

soft or hard

heavy or light

Safety First

God wants you to feel things that are safe. You must be very careful not to touch the wrong thing.

Remember:

1. Do not touch things that are very hot. Hot things can burn you. Never play with fire.

2. Never touch electric outlets. Be sure to keep your younger brother or sister from touching them, too.

3. Never touch things that are sharp. You will cut your skin if you touch things like a pin, knife, or saw.

Remember, whatever you are doing, it is important to be SAFE!

The Sense of Smelling

You can smell with your nose. God wants you to smell good things.

List 5 kinds of things you can smell.

1. _____

2. _____

3. _____

4. _____

5. _____

The Lord made your nose in a special way. Without your nose, you could not smell pretty flowers or nice food.

Your nose can also warn you of danger. If you smell smoke, there is often a fire!

I will praise You, for I am fearfully and wonderfully made....

PSALM 139:14A

SOMETHING YOU CAN DO

Draw pictures of things that you enjoy to see with your eyes, to hear with your ears, to taste with your tongue, to feel with your skin, and to smell with your nose. Draw these five things on the right side of the chart.

You may want to cut out pictures from magazines and paste them on the chart instead.

The Five Senses	Things I Love
I love to see . . .	
I love to hear . . .	
I love to taste . . .	
I love to feel . . .	
I love to smell . . .	

Caring for Your Body

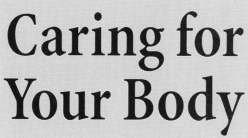

You must take good
care of your body
for God's glory.

Therefore,
whether you
eat or drink, or
whatever you do,
do all to the
glory of God.

1 CORINTHIANS 10:31

THINGS TO DO EVERYDAY

You must . . .

Wash each day
with soap and water.

Be sure to put on
clean clothes each day.

All boys and girls
must brush their teeth.

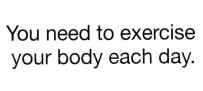

Keep your body
warm and dry.

You need to exercise
your body each day.

Be sure to get plenty
of rest each day.

Remember, God made you to love and serve Him.

WHAT A GOOD CHILD LOVES

I love the Lord who died for me,

I love His little child to be;

I love the Bible, where I find

How good my Savior was, and kind;

I love His people and their ways,

I love with them to pray and praise;

I love the Father and the Son,

And Holy Spirit, three in one;

I love to think the time will come

When I shall be in heaven my home.

Words to Know

dominion—to rule over something; in Genesis 1 God commanded man to rule over His creation

science—the study of God's creation

five senses—seeing, hearing, tasting, feeling, and smelling

heaven—the sky or the firmament above the earth; also a name for God's home

male—the name used for men and boys

female—the name used for women and girls

Looking Back

Circle true or false:

1. God made man in His own image.   true   false

2. The Lord does not like to plan things.   true   false

3. Each person was created with four senses.   true   false

4. It is bad to look directly at the sun.   true   false

5. Your tongue can taste things in four different ways.   true   false

6. Sometimes it is good to play with fire.   true   false

7. You smell things with your nose.   true   false

8. You hear things with your eyes.   true   false

9. God wants you to learn a lot about His creation.   true   false

— Chapter 8 —

STUDYING THINGS

Each part of
God's creation is different.

Some things are heavy.
Some things are light.

Why can these big ballons fly?
Because they are filled with hot air which is
lighter than the air around them.

Heavy or Light?

Every day we see things. Some things are heavy and some are light. Can you find some objects in the picture above that could be moved? Which of these objects would be the hardest to move? Which of these objects would be the easiest to move?

What is the heaviest object in this picture? What is the lightest? Why?

90

Looking at Things

Can you identify the things in each row below? If so, write a 1 on the line below the heaviest object in each row. Write a 2 on the line below the next heaviest object in each row. Write a 3 on the line below the next heaviest object, and 4 for the lightest object.

_____ _____ _____ _____

_____ _____ _____ _____

_____ _____ _____ _____

Complete the experiment on the next page to test yourself.

SOMETHING YOU CAN DO

You will need:

a **scale** to measure the **weight** of things, a block of wood, a sponge, a stack of books, and different-sized weights

Directions:

Weigh each of the objects by themselves. Place the first object on one side of the scale. Then place weights on the other side to make the scale level. The sum of the weights will tell you how much each object weighs.

Which object was the heaviest? Which object was the lightest? Paste a number 1 on the heaviest object. Paste a number 2 on the next heaviest object. Paste a number 3 on the lightest object.

PROJECT

A **balance** can help you tell which things are heavier and which things are lighter. If you follow the directions below, you can make your own balance and measure things.

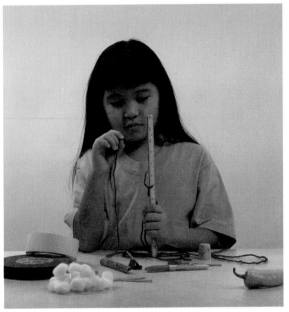

Take a strong ruler and tie a long string around the middle of the ruler. Next tie strings around each end of the ruler. Collect some small things to weigh (a spoon, a bottle of glue, an eraser, a pen, a small toy car, etc.). Tie two items, one at each end of the ruler; then lift the ruler up by the string in the middle.

The object that tips down farther is the heavier one. If both sides of the balance do not tip down, then both items weigh the same.

Sink or Float?

Some Things Sink . . .

Some Things Float . . .

Can you name the objects in the pictures above? Why do some things float? Why do some things sink?

Objects that are lighter than the top of the water will float. Things that are heavier will sink into the water.

SOMETHING TO DO

Finding things that sink or float

You will need:

A large glass bowl or **aquarium**; various small objects such as a pencil, spoon, cork, bottle, wooden block, and small rock.

Directions:

Put the object in the water and see if it stays on top of the water. Write down on paper the names of those objects that float and those that sink. Do some things float easier than others? Why?

Temperature of Things

Temperature is the measurement of how hot or cold something is. You can tell if something is hot or cold by using your fingers. If it is too hot you might burn yourself, so be careful! If it is too cold you might "burn" yourself, too! A safe way to find the temperature of things is by using a **thermometer**.

Write the word hot or cold under the correct picture.

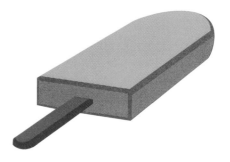

_____

_____

_____

_____

Warm or Cool?

Write the word warm or cool under the correct picture.

_____

_____

_____

_____

Can you name objects in your kitchen by their temperature?

Be careful not to touch something hot!

How Things Feel

Rough or Smooth?

Write the word rough or smooth under the correct picture.

_____ _____ _____ _____

Hard or Soft?

Write the word hard or soft under the correct picture.

_____ _____ _____ _____

Can you find any of the things listed above in your house? If so, ask your mom or dad if you can touch them to see how they feel. Be careful of rough objects!

Things Come in All Sizes

Tall or Short? Small or Large?

Write the word tall or short, small or large,

under the correct picture.

_____   _____   _____   _____

A **ruler** is a tool used to measure how long or tall something is. Ask your mom or dad to measure your **height**. How tall are you?

I am:_____ feet, _____ inches

Measure how tall your mom and dad are and write down their heights in the spaces below.

Mom: _____ feet, _____ inches

Dad: _____ feet, _____ inches

Ask your teacher to help you figure out how much shorter you are than your mother or father.

99

Words to Know

weight—the measurement of how heavy something is

scale—a tool used to measure the weight of things

balance—a tool used to tell if one object is heavier than another

aquarium—a "box" that has glass walls and can hold water; it is used to keep fish or other animals

temperature—the measurement of how hot or cold something is

thermometer—a tool used to measure the temperature of things

height—the measurement of how tall something is

ruler—a tool used to measure how long or tall something is

Looking Back

Circle true or false:

1. Each part of God's creation is different.   true   false

2. Things that are heavy are easy to move.   true   false

3. A scale is used to measure the weight of things.   true   false

4. Heavy items tend to sink rather than float.   true   false

5. A snowman would be a warm thing.   true   false

6. A bottle of milk would usually be cool.   true   false

7. A balloon is smooth to the touch.   true   false

8. A pillow is a very hard object.   true   false

9. The word tall and short mean the same thing.   true   false

10. An elephant is a large animal.   true   false

A Few Last Words

We hope that you have enjoyed your study of *Our Father's World*. It is our prayer that you will continue to study God's wonderful creation in the days ahead.

Most important of all, however, we pray that you will come to know God's Son, Christ Jesus, as your Savior. Through Christ, the world was made. All power in heaven and earth belongs to Him. He alone can give you wisdom for life on earth and for the world to come.

All things were made by God and for His glory. As you study His creation, therefore, be sure to worship the Creator alone.

Michael J. McHugh

In the beginning was
the Word,
and the Word was with God,
and the Word was God.

The same was in
the beginning with God.

All things were made by him;
and without him
was not anything made
that was made.

— John 1: 1-3 —